WORLD OF WORK

ARTS & COMMUNICATION

Exploring Career Pathways

Diane Lindsey Reeves

Created and produced by
Bright Futures Press, Cary, North Carolina
www.brightfuturespress.com

Published by
Cherry Lake Publishing, Ann Arbor, Michigan
www.cherrylakepublishing.com

Photo Credits: Cover, Beautyline; page 7, View Apart, Mike Focus, Juan Aunion, ProStockStudio, PR Image Factory, Speed Kingz, antb; steven r henricks; page 8, View Apart; page 10, Mike Focus; page 12, Juan Aunion; page 14, ProStockStudio; page 16, PR Image Factory; page 18, Speed Kingz; page 20, antb; page 22, steven r hendricks; page 24, balabolka.

Copyright @ 2018 by Bright Futures Press

All rights reserved. No part of this book may be reproduced or utilized in any form or by any means without written permission from the publisher.

Library of Congress Cataloging-in-Publication Date

Names: Reeves, Diane Lindsey, 1959- author.
Title: Arts & communication / by Diane Lindsey Reeves.
Other titles: Arts & Communication
Description: Cary, North Carolina : Bright Futures Press, 2017. | Series:
  World of work
Identifiers: LCCN 2017002769| ISBN 9781534101708 (hardcover) | ISBN
  9781534101784 (pdf) | ISBN 9781534101869 (pbk.) | ISBN 9781534101944
  (hosted ebook)
Subjects: LCSH: Performing arts--Vocational guidance--Juvenile literature. |
  Mass media--Vocational guidance--Juvenile literature.
Classification: LCC PN1580 .R44 2017 | DDC 791.023--dc23
LC record available at https://lccn.loc.gov/2017002769

Printed in the United States of America.

TABLE OF CONTENTS

Hello, World of Work 4

Take a Hike 6

WoW Up Close 7

    Actor 8

    Broadcast Meteorologist 10

    Choreographer 12

    Costume Designer 14

    Illustrator 16

    Music Teacher 18

    Sound Engineer 20

    Sports Photographer 22

WoW Big List 24

Take Your Pick 26

Explore Some More 27

My WoW 30

Glossary 31

Index 32

HELLO WORLD OF WORK

This is you.

Right now, your job is to go to school and learn all you can.

This is the world of work.

It's where people earn a living, find purpose in their lives, and make the world a better place.

Sooner or later, you'll have to find your way from HERE to THERE.

To get started, take all the jobs in the incredibly enormous world of work and organize them into an imaginary pile. It's a big pile, isn't it? It would be pretty tricky to find the perfect job for you among so many options.

No worries!

Some very smart career experts have made it easier to figure out. They sorted jobs and industries into groups by the types of skills and products they share. These groups are called career clusters. They provide pathways that will make it easier for you to find career options that match your interests.

- Architecture & Construction
- Arts & Communication
- Business & Administration
- Education & Training
- Finance
- Food & Natural Resources
- Government
- Health Sciences
- Hospitality & Tourism
- Human Services
- Information Technology
- Law & Public Safety
- Manufacturing
- Marketing, Sales & Service
- Science, Technology, Engineering & Mathematics (STEM)
- Transportation

Good thing you are still a kid.

You have lots of time to explore ideas and imagine yourself doing all kinds of amazing things. The **World of Work** (WoW for short) series of books will help you get started.

TAKE A HIKE!

There are 16 career pathways waiting for you to explore. The only question is: Which one should you explore first?

Is **Arts & Communication** a good path for you to start exploring career ideas? There is a lot to like about careers in the Arts & Communication. These professionals keep us entertained, informed, and in touch with the rest of the world. They star in our favorite movies. They report the news from wherever it happens. They write and illustrate the books we read for fun and for learning. And much, much more!

See if any of the following questions grab your interest.

WOULD YOU ENJOY drawing your own cartoons, using your smartphone to make a movie, or writing articles for the student newspaper?

CAN YOU IMAGINE someday working at a Hollywood movie studio, a publishing company, or a television news station?

ARE YOU CURIOUS ABOUT what actors, bloggers, graphic designers, museum curators, or writers do?

If so, it's time to take a hike! Keep reading to see what kinds of opportunities you can discover along the Arts & Communication pathway.

But wait!

What if you don't think you'll like this pathway?

You have two choices.

You could keep reading, to find out more than you already know. You might be surprised to learn how many amazing careers you'll find along this path.

OR

Turn to page 27 to get ideas about other WoW pathways.

SOUND ENGINEER

SPORTS PHOTOGRAPHER

COSTUME DESIGNER

LUSTRATOR

WoW Up Close

They report headline news. They sing. They dance. They create all kinds of art. They communicate through headline news, Hollywood movies, museum exhibits, and more. These are just some of the creative jobs that people who work along the Arts & Communication pathway do.

ACTOR

HOREOGRAPHER

BROADCAST METEOROLOGIST

MUSIC TEACHER

ACTOR

You see them in your favorite movies and television shows. You find them performing in Broadway plays. You spot them in commercials and music videos. They make you laugh, cry, and sit at the edge of your seat wondering what's going to happen next.

Who are they? They are **actors**!

Actors get paid to pretend to be someone else. Good actors do this so well you actually believe they are the character they play on-screen. An actor might play a lawyer in one show and a doctor in another. Sometimes they save the day as a hero, while other times they create turmoil as an evil villain. Each role requires an actor to look, talk, move, and behave in different ways. Sometimes, the transformation is so complete that an actor's mother can't recognize her own child!

Good actors make acting look easy. But it takes lots of skill, training, and talent to make it as an actor. Filming just one scene in a movie can require as many as 50 "**takes**" to get it right! Of course, just landing an acting job is hard work. Actors have to **audition** for every role, and there is a lot of competition. But, as they say, the show must go on!

Check It Out!

Check out some of your favorite actors at

▶ http://www.nick.com/kids-choice-awards

Or use the Internet to find out more about the stars of your favorite shows.

Start Now!

- ✓ Try out for a school or community play.
- ✓ Get some friends together to act out scenes from a favorite book.
- ✓ Practice expressing different emotions in front of a mirror.

BROADCAST METEOROLOGIST

Broadcast meteorologists are part scientist and part performer. As scientists, they have to know a lot about weather and earth science. As performers, they report weather news for television and radio broadcasts in ways that make people pay attention and understand.

On most days, broadcast meteorologists make life more comfortable for their viewers. Thanks to daily weather reports, people know if they need to wear a raincoat, sandals, or snow boots. They can be prepared for whatever Mother Nature brings that day.

Other days, when severe weather like hurricanes or tornados threaten an area, meteorologists actually save lives. They warn people to get out of harm's way and alert them to danger.

Every day, meteorologists report current weather conditions. They use special equipment to measure things like **temperature**, **humidity**, wind, and **precipitation**. Meteorologists also make weather **forecasts** and predict what they expect the weather will be like tomorrow, over the weekend, or next week. Computers, radar, and satellites help meteorologists collect data and gather clues.

Meteorologists also know how to observe trends and weather patterns. Sometimes all they have to do is look out the window to see if their predictions are right!

Check It Out!

Play around with the weather at

- http://youngmeteorologist.org
- http://climatekids.nasa.gov

Start Now!

- Be a weather watcher and compare your notes with an online or television weather report.
- Make a list of creative ways to describe the weather.
- Find out all you can about clouds and what they say about weather.

CHOREOGRAPHER

Have you ever watched music videos or Super Bowl halftime performances and wondered how all those dancers make the same moves at exactly the same time? Seriously! It's amazing to watch.

All of these entertaining acts start in the imagination of a **choreographer**.

Choreographers tell stories with dance. They turn music into movement. Their main job is to **compose** ballets and other types of dances by planning and arranging the movements, steps, and patterns of dancers. But their job isn't complete until they have taught the dance to the dancers.

Teaching other dancers how to dance means two things. First, it means that the choreographer is a great dancer, too. Sometimes telling dancers what to do is not enough. Choreographers have to show them how it is done—with just the right energy and emotion.

Second, it means lots and lots of practice. A dance routine may only last for a few minutes. But one dance can include many dozens of steps. And a Broadway play or ballet can have as many as a dozen songs in it. Do the math, and it is easy to see how it can take weeks or even months of practice and planning before a production is ready for an audience. Eventually, the music and the moves come together until there is no doubt…

It's showtime!

Check It Out!

Get acquainted with some famous choreographers at

➡ http://bit.ly/ FamousChoreographers

Learn how to choreograph a dance at

➡ http://bit.ly/ HowToChoreograph

Start Now!

- ✓ Make up a dance routine for your favorite song.
- ✓ Watch a music video and imitate the moves.
- ✓ Explore different types of dance like ballet, jazz, hip-hop, and shag.

COSTUME DESIGNER

So, you are filming a movie about the American Revolution. Your job is to do everything you can to take your viewers back in history to the 1700s. This includes dressing the characters in clothes that people wore back in the days of George Washington.

You'll need **waistcoats**, **breeches**, and **tricorn hats** for the men. Petticoats, **stays**, and pretty gowns for the women. And don't forget the powdered white wigs. Where will you find clothes like these? It's not like you can run out to Walmart and get them off the rack.

You are a **costume designer**! Some of the clothes you'll design and make yourself. Some of the clothes you'll borrow from through museums and collectors.

Costume designers do many of the same things that fashion designers do. They create fabulous clothes for people to wear. One big difference is that costume designers design wardrobes for characters to wear on-screen in movies or TV or onstage in theater plays. Another difference is that costume designers need to know as much about history as they do fashion. Depending on the project, they are just as likely to design clothes for a medieval knight as they are a modern-day teenager. Dressing every character for every scene is a big job, but getting it right makes the production come alive.

Check It Out!

Get your start as a costume designer by designing a Halloween costume for yourself or a younger sibling. Search online for ideas using the search terms "make your own Halloween costume."

Start Now!

- ✓ Volunteer to help make costumes for your next school play.

- ✓ Sketch out ideas for costumes for a movie about space aliens, kids your age, or fairy princesses.

- ✓ Make a timeline of the "history of fashion" from the year you were born until now. How have fashion trends changed over time?

ILLUSTRATOR

Think Mickey Mouse. Olivia. Snoopy. Pete the Cat. What images pop into your mind? Do you picture a talking mouse? A dancing pig? A beagle who hangs out with Charlie Brown and the gang? A troublemaking cat?

If so, it is because **illustrators** have done their jobs very well. They have used their artistic talents to create memorable characters that tell stories children want to read again and again.

Illustrators draw the pictures that are found in children's books, comic books, and cartoons. Some illustrators use pencils, pens, paints, and other materials to make their illustrations. Other illustrators use computer programs like Adobe Illustrator to do their artwork. Computers are especially useful when illustrating cartoons and other shows that use the same characters and scenes multiple times. Since a typical cartoon show can require more than 20,000 drawings, computers make it much easier to get the job done!

Besides entertaining children, illustrators also create original artwork for magazines, catalogs, and advertisements. They may specialize in fashion design, medical manuals, greeting cards, nature scenes, or other types of technical drawings.

No matter how they create their illustrations or where they are used, illustrators prove the old saying that a picture is worth a thousand words!

Check It Out!

Find out what illustrators do at

- http://bit.ly/illustratorA
- http://bit.ly/illustratorB
- http://bit.ly/IllustratorDo

Start Now!

- ✓ Use the Internet to find out more about a favorite children's book illustrator like Walt Disney, Dr. Seuss, or Maurice Sendak.

- ✓ Get a sketchbook and start drawing pictures of things you see around you.

- ✓ Illustrate a greeting card for your friend's birthday.

MUSIC TEACHER

Do-re-mi-fa-so-la-ti-do!

If you know how to sing this musical scale, you probably have a **music teacher** to thank. Music teachers work in elementary schools, middle schools, high schools, and colleges. They teach students how to sing, play instruments, and compose music.

Some teach music classes to each grade in a school. Others direct school bands, choirs, and orchestras.

All music teachers share one goal: to teach students to enjoy music. This can be a big challenge. Some students have natural musical talent and are eager to learn all they can. For other students, learning music can be as difficult as learning another language. They struggle to sing on key and follow a beat. Finding ways to meet the needs of both types of students—and all those in between—is what music teachers do every day.

Want to know what it's like to be a music teacher? Imagine you have a class of 20 kids who have never played a musical instrument. Give each student an instrument, such as a flute, clarinet, saxophone, violin, drums, cymbals, or other choice. Now, work with them every day for an entire school year. There will be days you'll wish you had earplugs. Somewhere along the line, however, real music starts happening. That's when you know you've done your job!

Check It Out!

Enjoy some musical fun and games at

- http://www.sfskids.org
- http://www.nyphilkids.org
- http://www.classicsforkids.com

Start Now!

- ✓ Join the kids' choir at your school or place of worship.
- ✓ Make a list of your top 10 songs.
- ✓ See what kinds of musical instruments you can create using stuff you find around the house.

SOUND ENGINEER

What does a **sound engineer** do? Professional sound engineers operate and maintain sound recording or broadcasting equipment. They work with musical artists, movie directors, television news stations, and radio stations. The goal of this profession is to ensure that any recording or broadcast has high-quality, crystal-clear sound.

Some sound engineers work in recording studios or sound booths. They sit in control booths with lots of equipment for recording, editing, and mixing music. When working with musicians, they use microphones to pick up and separate the sounds made by both the musicians and the musical instruments. When working with actors or news broadcasts, they mix the sounds from different actors or anchors, special effects, and background noises. In both cases, their job involves unfolding the sounds layer by layer to mix and balance them in the best possible way.

Other sound engineers work the sound boards at live events such as concerts, plays, and other theater performances. Similar types of equipment are used for these events. The big difference is that these sound engineers have to get the sound right the first time. There is no time for editing and no second chances during a live show!

Check It Out!

Compare the differences between live and recording sound engineers at

- http://bit.ly/SoundLive
- http://bit.ly/SoundRecord

Start Now!

- Volunteer to help the DJ at the next school dance.
- Use a smartphone or digital recorder to make a recording of your family or friends singing bits of a favorite song.
- Digital recordings are big now, but your parents and grandparents listened to music in different ways. See what you can find out about vinyl records, cassette tapes, and 8-track tapes.

SPORTS PHOTOGRAPHER

It's game time. Your number one team is squaring off against its number one rival. You don't want to miss a minute of the action. The only problem is that the game is happening at a college that is hundreds of miles away.

No problem! Thanks to cable television and some talented **sports photographers**, you won't miss a single play. Capturing all the action at a major sporting event takes a lot of skill and much fancier equipment than your parents use to record your games.

For instance, 70 different cameras were used to record all the action at the 2016 Super Bowl. This included some really cool camera technology such as aerial cameras—called Sky Cams— pylon cameras, and special replay cameras. The photographers who use these high-tech cameras have to know their stuff and be able to think fast in order to catch the most exciting happenings on a huge football field.

Sports photographers need to know a lot about the sport they are covering. It is probably safe to assume that most of them are huge sports fans! But they are also skilled and talented camera operators.

Check It Out!

Check out the latest news about your favorite sports teams at

▶ https://www.sikids.com

Watch all kinds of sports events live online at

▶ http://watchsports.live

Start Now!

- ✓ Use a smartphone or digital camera to record all the action at your school's next sports event.

- ✓ Watch sports events on television or online and notice all the different angles covered by the cameras.

- ✓ Go online and find tips about "how to film sports events." Make a poster to share what you learn.

3-D animator • Account manager • **ACTOR** • Aerial specialist • Agent • Anchor • Animator • Archivist • Art director • Art teacher • Artist • Artist representative • Artistic director • Assignment editor • Audiovisual equipment technician • Audiovisual specialist • Author • Best boy • Boom operator • Brand manager • Broadcast engineer • **BROADCAST METEOROLOGIST** • Broadcast news technician • Business manager • Camera operator • Casting director • Chief digital officer • **CHOREOGRAPHER** • Commercial designer • Computer

WoW Big List

Take a look at some of the different kinds of jobs people do in the Arts & Communication pathway. **WoW!**

Some of these job titles will be familiar to you. Others will be so unfamiliar that you will scratch your head and say "huh?"

programmer • Conservator • Copy editor • Correspondent • **COSTUME DESIGNER** • Court reporter • Craft artist • Creative director • Curator • Dancer • Desktop publisher • Director • Disc jockey (DJ) • Drama teacher • Editor • Engraver • Etcher • Fashion designer • Film and video editor • Fine artist • Foley artist • Gaffer • Graphic designer • Historian • Home entertainment system installer • **ILLUSTRATOR** • Industrial designer • Interior designer • Lighting designer • Location scout • Lyricist • Makeup artist • Managing editor • Media buyer • Multimedia artist • Museum collections manager • Music composer • Music director • **MUSIC TEACHER** • Musician • News director • Painter • Photographer • Photojournalist • Poet • Prepress technician • Printer binder • Printing prepress operator • Producer • Program director • Proofreader • Property master • Publisher • Radio operator • Recording engineer • Reporter • Sculptor • Set designer

Find a job title that makes you curious. Type the name of the job into your favorite Internet search engine and find out more about the people who have that job.

1. What do they do?
2. Where do they work?
3. How much training do they need to do this job?

• Singer • Songwriter • Sound editor • Social media editor • **SOUND ENGINEER** • Special effects technician • Sports director • **SPORTS PHOTOGRAPHER** • Stagehand • Stage manager • Stunt performer • Talent director • Technical writer • Telecommunications equipment installer • татары TV news anchor • TV station manager • Videographer • Web content writer • Writer

TAKE YOUR PICK

	Put stars next to your 3 favorite career ideas	Put an X next to the career idea you like the least	Put a question mark next to the career idea you want to learn more about
Actor			
Broadcast meteorologist			
Choreographer			
Costume designer			
Illustrator			
Music teacher			
Sound engineer			
Sports photographer			
	What do you like most about these careers?	What is it about this career that doesn't appeal to you?	What do you want to learn about this career? Where can you find answers?

Which Big Wow List ideas are you curious about?

Please do **NOT** write in this book if it doesn't belong to you. You can download a copy of this activity online at www.brightfuturespress.com/teacher-guides.

EXPLORE SOME MORE

The Arts & Communication pathway is only one of 16 career pathways that hold exciting options for your future. Take a look at the other 15 to figure out where to start exploring next.

Architecture & Construction

WOULD YOU ENJOY making things with LEGOs™, building a treehouse or birdhouse, or designing the world's best skate park?

CAN YOU IMAGINE someday working at a construction site, a design firm, or a building company?

ARE YOU CURIOUS ABOUT what civil engineers, demolition technicians, heavy-equipment operators, landscape architects, or urban planners do?

Business & Administration

WOULD YOU ENJOY playing Monopoly, being the boss of your favorite club or team, or starting your own business?

CAN YOU IMAGINE someday working at a big corporate headquarters, government agency, or international business center?

ARE YOU CURIOUS ABOUT what brand managers, chief executive officers, e-commerce analysts, entrepreneurs, or purchasing agents do?

Education & Training

WOULD YOU ENJOY babysitting, teaching your grandparents how to use a computer, or running a summer camp for neighbor kids in your backyard?

CAN YOU IMAGINE someday working at a college counseling center, corporate training center, or school?

ARE YOU CURIOUS ABOUT what animal trainers, coaches, college professors, guidance counselors, or principals do?

Finance

WOULD YOU ENJOY earning and saving money, being the class treasurer, or playing the stock market game?

CAN YOU IMAGINE someday working at an accounting firm, bank, or Wall Street stock exchange?

ARE YOU CURIOUS ABOUT what accountants, bankers, fraud investigators, property managers, or stockbrokers do?

Food & Natural Resources

WOULD YOU ENJOY exploring nature, growing your own garden, or setting up a recycling center at your school?

CAN YOU IMAGINE someday working at a national park, raising crops in a city farm, or studying food in a laboratory?

ARE YOU CURIOUS ABOUT what landscape architects, chefs, food scientists, environmental engineers, or forest rangers do?

Government

WOULD YOU ENJOY reading about U.S. presidents, running for student council, or helping a favorite candidate win an election?

CAN YOU IMAGINE someday working at a chamber of commerce, government agency, or law firm?

ARE YOU CURIOUS about what mayors, customs agents, federal special agents, intelligence analysts, or politicians do?

Health Sciences

WOULD YOU ENJOY nursing a sick pet back to health, dissecting animals in a science lab, or helping the school coach run a sports clinic?

CAN YOU IMAGINE someday working at a dental office, hospital, or veterinary clinic?

ARE YOU CURIOUS ABOUT what art therapists, doctors, dentists, pharmacists, and veterinarians do?

Hospitality & Tourism

WOULD YOU ENJOY traveling, sightseeing, or meeting people from other countries?

CAN YOU IMAGINE someday working at a convention center, resort, or travel agency?

ARE YOU CURIOUS ABOUT what convention planners, golf pros, tour guides, resort managers, or wedding planners do?

Human Services

WOULD YOU ENJOY showing a new kid around your school, organizing a neighborhood food drive, or being a peer mediator?

CAN YOU IMAGINE someday working at an elder care center, fitness center, or mental health center?

ARE YOU CURIOUS ABOUT what elder care center directors, hairstylists, personal trainers, psychologists, or religious leaders do?

Information Technology

WOULD YOU ENJOY creating your own video game, setting up a Web site, or building your own computer?

CAN YOU IMAGINE someday working at an information technology start-up company, software design firm, or research and development laboratory?

ARE YOU CURIOUS ABOUT what artificial intelligence scientists, big data analysts, computer forensic investigators, software engineers, or video game designers do?

Law & Public Safety

WOULD YOU ENJOY working on the school safety patrol, participating in a mock court trial at school, or coming up with a fire escape plan for your home?

CAN YOU IMAGINE someday working at a cyber security company, fire station, police department, or prison?

ARE YOU CURIOUS ABOUT what animal control officers, coroners, detectives, firefighters, or park rangers do?

Manufacturing

WOULD YOU ENJOY figuring out how things are made, competing in a robot-building contest, or putting model airplanes together?

CAN YOU IMAGINE someday working at a high-tech manufacturing plant, engineering firm, or global logistics company?

ARE YOU CURIOUS ABOUT what chemical engineers, industrial designers, supply chain managers, robotics technologists, or welders do?

Marketing, Sales & Service

WOULD YOU ENJOY keeping up with the latest fashion trends, picking favorite TV commercials during Super Bowl games, or making posters for a favorite school club?

CAN YOU IMAGINE someday working at an advertising agency, corporate marketing department, or retail store?

ARE YOU CURIOUS ABOUT what creative directors, market researchers, media buyers, retail store managers, and social media consultants do?

Science, Technology, Engineering & Mathematics (STEM)

WOULD YOU ENJOY concocting experiments in a science lab, trying out the latest smartphone, or taking advanced math classes?

CAN YOU IMAGINE someday working in a science laboratory, engineering firm, or research and development center?

ARE YOU CURIOUS ABOUT what aeronautical engineers, ecologists, statisticians, oceanographers, or zoologists do?

Transportation

WOULD YOU ENJOY taking pilot or sailing lessons, watching a NASA rocket launch, or helping out in the school carpool lane?

CAN YOU IMAGINE someday working at an airport, mass transit system, or shipping port?

ARE YOU CURIOUS ABOUT what air traffic controllers, flight attendants, logistics planners, surveyors, and traffic engineers do?

MY WoW

I am here.

Name

Grade

School

Who I am.

Make a word collage! Use 5 adjectives to form a picture that describes who you are.

Where I'm going.

The next career pathway I want to explore is

_____

Some things I need to learn first to succeed.

1 _____

2 _____

3 _____

My Career Choice

To get here.

Please do **NOT** write in this book if it doesn't belong to you. You can download a copy of this activity online at www.brightfuturespress.com/teacher-guides.

GLOSSARY

actor
person who performs in movies, on television, or on the stage

arts
the various types of creative activity, such as painting, music, literature, and dance

audition
give a short performance to test whether you are right for a specific role

breeches
knee-length trousers, often having ornamental buckles or elaborate decorations at or near the bottoms, commonly worn by men and boys in the 17th, 18th, and early 19th centuries

broadcast meteorologist
scientist who reports and forecasts weather conditions on television and radio

choreographer
person who composes the sequence of steps and moves for a dance performance

communication
sharing information by speaking, writing, or using some other means such as television or the Internet

compose
to write or create a work of art such as music, poetry, or dance

costume designer
person who designs wardrobes for characters to wear in movies, TV, or plays

forecasts
predictions of future weather conditions

humidity
the amount of moisture in the air

illustrator
person who draws or creates pictures for magazines, books, advertising, or other purposes

music teacher
person who teaches people how to play a musical instrument or gives singing or voice lessons, either privately or in a school

petticoats
women's skirt-like garments worn under or over gowns

precipitation
water that falls to the ground as rain, snow, or sleet

sound engineer
person who is responsible for the technical aspects of a sound recording, broadcast, or musical performance

sports photographer
person who films the action at a sporting event

stays
corset-like undergarments worn by women in the 18th century

takes
filmed versions of a scene or shots of a movie or television show

temperature
the degree of hotness or coldness that can be measured by a thermometer

tricorn hats
hats having the brim turned up on three sides, popular in the 18th century

waistcoats
men's quilted long-sleeved garments worn under short, close-fitting jackets in the 16th and 17th centuries

INDEX

American Revolution, 14

Architecture & Construction, 5, 27

Arts & Communication, 5

Biography.com, 13

Business & Administration, 5, 27

*Chapman, Lynne, 17

Charlie Brown, 16

*Classics for Kids, 19

Disney, Walt, 17

Dr. Seuss, 17

Education & Training, 5, 27

Finance, 5, 27

Food & Natural Resources, 5, 28

Government, 5, 28

Health Science, 5, 28

Hospitality & Tourism 5, 28

*HowStuffWorks, 21

Human Resources, 5, 28

Information Technology, 5, 28

Law & Public Safety, 5, 29

Manufacturing, 5, 29

Marketing, Sales & Service, 5, 29

Mickey Mouse, 16

Mother Nature, 11

*NASA Climate Kids, 11

*New York Philharmonic, 19

*Nickelodeon Kids' Choice Awards, 9

Olivia, 16

Pete the Cat, 16

*San Francisco Symphony, 19

Science, Technology, Engineering & Mathematics, 5, 29

Sendak, Maurice, 17

Snoopy, 16

Super Bowl, 12

*Tolson, Sarah, 17

Transportation, 5, 29

*Valencia, Rizaldy, 17

Walmart, 15

Washington, George, 14

*Wikihow, 13

*Young Meteorologists, 11

* Refers to the Web page sources

About the Author

Diane Lindsey Reeves is the author of lots of children's books. She has written several original PEANUTS stories (published by Regnery Kids and Sourcebooks). She is especially curious about what people do and likes to write books that get kids thinking about all the cool things they can be when they grow up. She lives in Cary, North Carolina, and her favorite thing to do is play with her grandkids—Conrad, Evan, Reid, and Hollis Grace.